DOMINOES

D0602802

Kidnap!

STARTER LEVEL   **250 HEADWORDS**

OXFORD
UNIVERSITY PRESS

Great Clarendon Street, Oxford OX2 6DP

Oxford University Press is a department of the University of Oxford.
It furthers the University's objective of excellence in research, scholarship,
and education by publishing worldwide in

Oxford New York

Auckland Cape Town Dar es Salaam Hong Kong Karachi
Kuala Lumpur Madrid Melbourne Mexico City Nairobi
New Delhi Shanghai Taipei Toronto

With offices in

Argentina Austria Brazil Chile Czech Republic France Greece
Guatemala Hungary Italy Japan Poland Portugal Singapore
South Korea Switzerland Thailand Turkey Ukraine Vietnam

OXFORD and OXFORD ENGLISH are registered trade marks of
Oxford University Press in the UK and in certain other countries

This edition © Oxford University Press 2010

The moral rights of the author have been asserted

Database right Oxford University Press (maker)

First published in Dominoes 2005

2014 2013 2012 2011 2010

10 9 8 7 6 5 4 3 2 1

ISBN: 978 0 19 424711 5 BOOK
ISBN: 978 0 19 424675 0 BOOK AND MULTIROM PACK
MULTIROM NOT AVAILABLE SEPARATELY

No unauthorized photocopying

Printed in China

ACKNOWLEDGEMENTS

Illustrations by: Maya Gavin

The publisher would like to thank the following for permission to reproduce photographs: Corbis p24
(limousine/Rick Gomez); Getty Images pp19 (driving in snow/Philip Condit/Photographer's
Choice), 25 (classroom/Rod Morata/Stone+); OUP p6 (mobile phone).

DOMINOES

Series Editors: Bill Bowler and Sue Parminter

Kidnap!

John Escott

Illustrated by Maya Gavin

John Escott has written many books for readers of all ages, and particularly enjoys writing crime and mystery thrillers. He was born in the west of England, but now lives on the south coast. When he is not writing, he visits second-hand bookshops, watches videos of old Hollywood movies, and takes long walks along empty beaches. He has also written *The Wild West*, *A Pretty Face*, *Kidnap!* and *The Big Story*, and retold *William Tell and Other Stories* for Dominoes.

OXFORD
UNIVERSITY PRESS

BEFORE READING

This is Tom. He's an artist and he lives in the United States. One day he goes to a bookstore. What happens? Tick the boxes.

a At the bookstore Tom finds . . .

   1 a cell phone   **2** a gun   **3** a map

b He gets . . .

   1 a book   **2** a coffee   **3** a magazine

c He draws a picture of . . .

   1 an interesting woman   **2** a movie star   **3** a police officer

d He sees two men. They are . . .

   1 bodyguards   **2** kidnappers   **3** movie stars

Kidnap!

CHAPTER 1

Tom lives in America, near the town of Harper. He is an **artist** and he works at home. He is working on a **comic strip**.

'How do the two friends **escape**?' Tom thinks. 'They're running through some trees, and a man with a **gun** is running after them. I need a new **idea**.'

artist a person who makes pictures

comic strip a story with pictures

escape to get away from something bad

gun a person can fight with this

idea something that you think

'**Maybe** I need to go out,' Tom thinks.

It's **winter** and there's a lot of **snow**. 'I can go to the **bookstore** in Harper,' Tom thinks. 'It's warm in there.'

'I need some **coffee**,' he thinks. He **parks** his car and goes into the bookstore.

maybe perhaps

winter the time of year when it is very cold

snow something soft, cold and white

bookstore a shop for books

coffee people often drink this in the morning

park to stop driving and leave your car

Tom goes to the coffee shop in the bookstore.

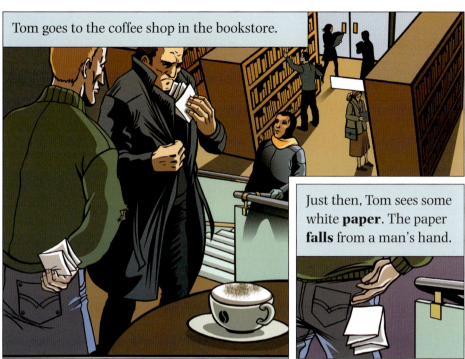

Just then, Tom sees some white **paper**. The paper **falls** from a man's hand.

'Wait!' Tom calls. 'This is yours!'
But the man doesn't hear him. Tom looks at the paper. It has a **map** on it. He puts the paper into his coat. 'Maybe it's not important,' he thinks.

He gets a cup of coffee, and sits down at a table.

paper you write on this   **fall** to go down suddenly   **map** a picture that shows where things are

3

Tom sees a woman with red hair at a table near him.
'That's an interesting face,' he thinks. 'I'd like to **draw** it, but I don't have any paper.'
Then he remembers the man's map. 'Oh! Yes, I do!'

Tom finishes the picture of the woman. He's happy with it.

'Maybe I can use this in a comic strip,' he thinks.

Tom drinks his coffee and goes down into the bookstore. He looks out of the window and sees the woman from the coffee shop.
'Is something wrong?' he thinks. 'Why is she standing there in the street?'

draw to make a picture with a pen or pencil

Tom goes out to the street.
'Hi! Are you OK?' Tom asks.
'It's my car,' the woman says.
'There's something wrong with it.'

Tom wants to help the woman.
'You need to call a **tow truck**,' he says. 'They can come and get your car. Here's my **cell phone**.'

'What's that?' the woman asks, when she sees Tom's picture.
'It . . . it's a picture of you,' Tom says. 'I'm an artist. I draw pictures for comic books. Oh, but there's a map—'

Tom tells the woman about the men in the bookstore. They look at the map. 'Look at this!' says Tom, and he reads from the map.

A AND J-A ARRIVE AT 12.30pm, MAYBE WITH BODYGUARD VAN WAITS HERE   H-SCHOOL

CAR COMES ACROSS ROAD HERE. WE GET AWAY WITH A IN THE VAN,

57

tow truck a big car that can pull your car when it isn't working

cell phone a phone that you carry with you

bodyguard a strong person who protects famous people

van a big car, with no side windows at the back

READING CHECK

Choose the right words to complete the sentences.

a Tom is an artist. At home he is working on a . . .
1 ☐ big picture.
2 ☑ comic strip.
3 ☐ map.

b Tom goes to the . . .
1 ☐ supermarket.
2 ☐ airport.
3 ☐ bookstore.

c Tom sees a . . . fall from a man's hand.
1 ☐ map
2 ☐ photo
3 ☐ gun

d Tom draws a picture of . . .
1 ☐ an old woman.
2 ☐ an interesting woman.
3 ☐ a man and a woman.

e There's something wrong with the woman's . . .
1 ☐ car.
2 ☐ cell phone.
3 ☐ coffee.

f On the map Tom and the woman read about . . .
1 ☐ a bodyguard and a van.
2 ☐ a bodyguard and a plane.
3 ☐ a van and a plane.

WORD WORK

Use the words in the cell phone to complete the sentences.

a Tom must think of a new . . . . idea . . . . for his story.

b In the . . . . it's very cold and sometimes there's a lot of . . . . on the hills.

c There's something wrong with our car. We need to call a . . . .

d 'Can you do the English homework?' '. . . . . I can, but it's difficult!'

escape idea
maybe van
winter snow
park paper
fall comic strip
tow truck

Send   Discard

e Please write your phone number on this . . . .

f He has a gun! How can we . . . . from him?

g You can . . . . your car in front of the bookstore.

h Be careful! Don't . . . . down from there.

i *Garfield* is a very good . . . . about a fat cat.

j Our gardener drives a big green . . . . with his name on it.

GUESS WHAT

What happens in the next chapter? Read the sentences and write *Yes* or *No*.

a Tom says goodbye to the woman. Then he goes home.   . . . . . .

b Tom talks to the woman. The two men from the bookstore want to kidnap somebody, he tells her.   . . . . . .

c Tom and the woman take the map to the police.   . . . . . .

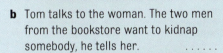

d Tom and the woman see a school on the map. They go to find the school in Tom's car.   . . . . . .

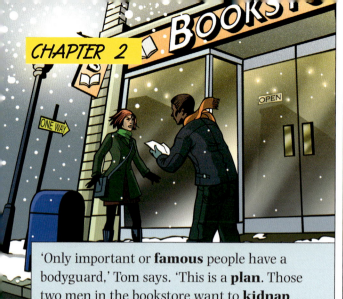

CHAPTER 2

'Only important or **famous** people have a bodyguard,' Tom says. 'This is a **plan**. Those two men in the bookstore want to **kidnap** somebody – "A"! And look. It says "H school". Maybe they want to kidnap a child.'

The woman gives a little laugh.
'Kidnap a child? You read a lot of comic books!' she says.

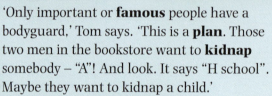

'This isn't a comic strip, this is **real life**,' says Tom. 'We must call the **police**.'
'Wait!' says the woman.
'Can I see the map again?'

'My name's Rita,' the woman says.
'What's your name?'
'Tom,' he tells her.
'Look, Tom. Maybe we can find the school first. Then we can ask the teachers, "Do you have any famous children here?" before we call the police.'

famous when many people know a person

plan when you get something ready to do later

kidnap to take someone away when they don't want to go

real life things that happens every day

police men and women who stop people doing bad things

In Boston, a famous mother and her daughter leave their house. The mother is Jodie-Anne Ryan, the **movie star**. The girl is Anastasia. She is thirteen years old.

'Why are we going to your old school?' Anastasia asks her mother.
'It's the winter **holiday concert**,' Jodie-Anne says. 'The students are singing and we must be there. They're singing for us.'
'Holiday concert? Oh, no! Mom, I want to go home now!'

'Please Anastasia, you must come with me. The students want to see you,' Jodie-Anne says.
'Well, I don't want to see *them*. Holiday concerts are **boring**!' Anastasia says.

movie star a famous person that you can see in moving pictures

holiday concert a school event in which the students sing and play music in front of other people

boring not interesting

9

Tom wants to call the police. 'There are no street names on the map,' he says. 'How can we find the school?'

'Maybe I know it,' Rita tells him. 'Come on, Tom. We can take your car.'

'What about your car?' Tom asks. 'Do you want to call the tow truck?'

'There isn't time,' Rita says. 'And this is more important than my car.'

'Go left at the next street,' Rita says. 'What time is it?' Tom asks. '**Almost** eleven-thirty,' Rita tells him.

'Only an hour before the kidnap,' Tom says. 'Are you **sure** about the school?' 'Uh – almost sure,' Rita says.

'Oh! There's **ice** on the road,' Tom says. 'Be careful!' she says.

almost nearly

sure when you feel something is true

ice water that is hard when it is very cold

ACTIVITIES

READING CHECK

Are these sentences true or false? Tick the boxes.   **True**   **False**

a The two men want to kidnap a child, Tom thinks.   ☑   ☐

b Tom calls the police.   ☐   ☐

c Rita wants to find the school.   ☐   ☐

d Jodie-Anne Ryan is a movie star.   ☐   ☐

e Anastasia wants to go to the holiday concert.   ☐   ☐

f Tom can see some street names on the map.   ☐   ☐

g There's only one hour before the kidnap.   ☐   ☐

h There's a lot of water on the road.   ☐   ☐

WORD WORK

1 Find ten words from Chapter 2 on the map.

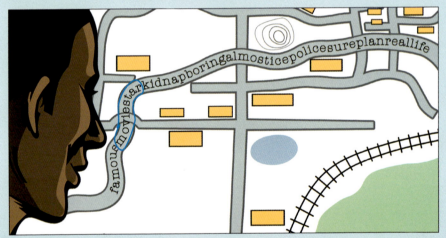

2 Use the words from Activity 1 to complete these sentences.

a 'Who's that beautiful woman in the long dress?' 'She's a Hollywood . . . movie . . . . star . . . . . '

b 'What's the time?' 'I'm not . . . . Maybe it's about two o'clock.'

c I don't want to read this book. It's very long and . . . .

d Look! There's a man with a gun. We must call the . . . . now!

e 'How old are you?' 'Twelve, but I'm . . . . thirteen. It's my birthday tomorrow.'

12

f She has a bodyguard because somebody wants to . . . . her.

g In the movie she has long dark hair but in . . . . she has short red hair.

h We have a . . . . We want to go to New York next weekend.

i I'd like a cold drink. Can you put some . . . . in it, please?

j That man in the red shirt is very . . . . Everybody knows him.

GUESS WHAT

What happens in the next chapter? Tick the boxes.

a Tom and Rita stop because they want to get . . .

1 a magazine.

2 some gas.

3 some lunch.

b Tom and Rita . . .

1 find the name of the school on the map.

2 can't find the school.

3 meet the two men from the bookstore.

CHAPTER 3

After twenty minutes, Tom says, 'I need some **gas**.'

GAS AND SHOP

'I can get some here,' Tom says. '**Hurry**,' Rita tells him. 'There isn't much time.'

'What time is it?' asks Tom again. 'It's almost twelve o'clock,' Rita says.

PUMP **3**

SHOP

PUMP **1**

W. JAMES PLUMBING

gas gasoline or petrol; cars need this to work

hurry to do something quickly

On a country road, the two men from the bookstore are looking at the map. 'The school's not far from here, Joe,' the big man says. 'Where's your map?' 'I don't know,' Joe says.

'I'm **worried**, Max,' Joe says. 'Where's the **boss**?' 'Listen, everything's OK,' Max tells him. 'Think of all the money, Joe!'

'Here, take my map, Joe. Drive down this road for five kilometres. There's a **place** to park on the right. Wait there, and be ready to move quickly when you see the car. Remember, it's a long, black car.'

worried not happy about something and thinking about it a lot

boss the person that you work for

place where something is

At the gas station, Tom pays for the gas. 'Hi,' he says to the girl in the shop. 'We're looking for a school near here.'

Tom **shows** her the map. 'Do you know this place?' he asks.
The girl looks at the map. 'I think . . .' she begins.

'What?' says Tom. 'Do you know it?' 'Maybe it's Bridgewater, a little town about three kilometres from here,' she says.

'Is there a school in Bridgewater?' Tom asks. 'Oh, yes,' the girl says. 'Hillside School.'

show to help someone to see something

Rita is waiting. 'What's he doing?' she thinks.

The girl shows Tom a **magazine**. There is a picture of a movie star on the front of the magazine.
'Do you know this woman?' she asks.
'Sure! It's Jodie-Anne Ryan!' says Tom.

'That's right,' the girl says. 'She's an old Hillside student. And that's her daughter – Anastasia.'

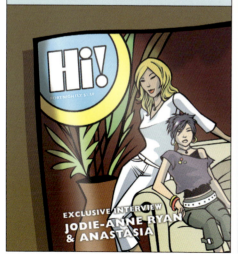

'Anastasia!' Tom thinks. '"A" for Anastasia! They want to kidnap Jodie-Anne Ryan's daughter!'

magazine a thin book with lots of pictures in it; you can buy it every week or every month

ACTIVITIES

READING CHECK

Choose the correct words to complete the sentences.

a Tom needs some (gas) money .

b Joe can't find his car map .

c Joe feels very happy worried .

d Joe and Max are waiting for the police their boss .

e Joe must look for a blue van black car .

f Tom Rita goes into the gas station.

g The girl shows Tom a map magazine .

h The men want to kidnap Anastasia Jodie-Anne , Tom thinks.

WORD WORK

Use the words in the papers to complete the sentences.

a 'It's fifty kilometres to the next town.'
'We must stop here and get some gas .' *sag*

b 'What's the matter?'
'I'm _ _ _ _ _ _ _ because I can't find my bag.' *owrirde*

c 'It's 8 o'clock. We're late!'
'Oh no! We must _ _ _ _ _ .' *ruryh*

d 'Do you like your new _ _ _ _?'
'Yes, she's very nice. We can leave work early every Friday now!' *sbso*

e 'Look, there's a photo of Jodie-Anne Ryan on the front of that _ _ _ _ _ _ _ _ .'
'I know! She's my favourite movie-star.' *gamaenzi*

f 'Do you know a good _ _ _ _ _ to have coffee?'
'Yes. Let's go to the bookstore.' *lcaep*

g 'Where do you live?'
'I can _ _ _ _ you on this map.' *hwos*

GUESS WHAT

What happens in the next chapter? Tick two answers.

a ☐ Tom finds Anastasia at the school.

b ☐ Tom tells the police about the kidnap plan.

c ☐ Rita takes out a gun.

d ☐ Tom and Rita meet Max.

CHAPTER 4

Rita sees Tom. He's running to the car. 'What's happening?' she thinks.

'They want to kidnap Anastasia, Jodie-Anne Ryan's daughter!' Tom says. 'Jodie-Anne Ryan – the movie star?' says Rita. 'Are you **kidding**?' 'We must call the police now,' Tom says.

'Oh, no! My cell phone's dead,' Tom says. 'Do you have a cell phone?'

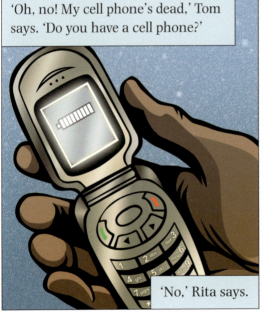

'No,' Rita says.

'I know! Let's call from the shop. You stay here and be ready to drive to the school.'

kid to say something that is not true

Rita runs to the shop.
'Hurry!' Tom says.

Tom **throws** his phone into the back of the car. He sees Rita's coat. Then he sees something in her coat **pocket**.

'What's this?' Tom says. 'It's— it's the map! She has it, too!'

'And she *has* a cell phone!' Tom says. 'So . . . who is she calling now? Is it the police, or . . . ?' He looks at the map.

throw to make something move from your hand through the air

pocket the place in your coat where you can put things

'No!' he thinks.
'She's phoning the
kidnappers! *She's* a
kidnapper, too!'

Rita gets into the car. She has a gun in her hand.
'You're—' Tom begins.
'Drive!' she tells Tom.

'Where are we going?' Tom asks.
'Don't ask **stupid** questions, Mr **Smart-guy**.
Drive!' Rita says.
She smiles, but it isn't a nice smile. 'And
when I say take a left, take a left.'

stupid not thinking well   **smart** quick-thinking   **guy** man

Tom drives carefully in the snow.

'Why do you want Jodie-Anne Ryan's daughter?' he asks Rita.

'Anastasia?' Rita says. 'We kidnap her, then we ask Jodie-Anne for three million dollars. She gives us the money and we give her Anastasia.'

'The police—' Tom begins.

'The police aren't coming,' Rita says, laughing. 'But my friends are waiting for us.'

After driving for ten minutes, Tom stops behind a blue van. 'Now we wait with Max,' Rita says. 'Get out.'

'Hello, Boss,' Max says to Rita.

READING CHECK

Put these sentences in the correct order. Number them 1–7.

a ☐ Rita gets into Tom's car with a gun.

b ☐ Tom stops behind a blue van.

c ☐ Tom and Rita meet Max.

d ☐ Tom tells Rita about the plan to kidnap Anastasia.

e ☐ Tom sees a map in Rita's pocket.

f ☐ Rita goes to phone from the shop.

g ☐ Tom finds Rita's cell phone.

WORD WORK

Use the words in the car to complete the sentences below.

kidding   throw   pocket
stupid   smart   guy

a That's not true! You're . . . kidding . . .

b Our son is very . . . . He's only two years old and he knows fifty words.

c Quick, I must call the police! Can you . . . . your cell phone to me, please?

d Don't lose your money. Put it in your . . . . now.

e It's a . . . . idea to go for a walk today. It's cold and it's raining.

f Do you know that . . . . over there? What's he doing?

GUESS WHAT

What happens in the next chapter? Tick the boxes.

		Yes	No
a	Rita, Max and Joe kidnap Anastasia.	☐	☐
b	Rita, Max and Joe want to kidnap Anastasia, but she escapes.	☐	☐
c	Jodie-Anne's bodyguard shoots Joe in the leg.	☐	☐
d	Joe kills Jodie-Anne's bodyguard.	☐	☐
e	The kidnappers put Anastasia and Tom in the blue van.	☐	☐
f	Anastasia drives the blue van away.	☐	☐

CHAPTER 5

Just then, a big black car comes down the road. 'Here they come,' Rita says.

'Almost there, Anastasia,' Jodie-Anne Ryan says. 'My old school is down this road.'
'Oh, **great**!' Anastasia says. 'And when can we go home?'

Suddenly, everything happens!

'Give me the girl!' Max **shouts** at Jodie-Anne.
'No!' **screams** the movie star. 'No, please don't take her.'

great very good

shout to say loudly and angrily

scream to give a loud high cry because you are afraid

Tom is in the back of the van. He can only watch.
'Get in the van!' Rita tells the girl.

Rita gets in the back, too, and Joe closes the doors. Max hurries to the front of the van.

Suddenly, Jodie-Anne's bodyguard takes a gun from under his coat.
'Be careful, Joe!' shouts Max.

The bodyguard **shoots** at Joe and hits him.
Joe screams, 'My leg!'

shoot to use a gun

'Joe's **hurt**!' Max shouts to Rita.
'Drive!' Rita tells him.

Max drives away – fast.
The bodyguard shoots but he can't
stop the van.

'Be careful, Max!' Rita shouts. 'There's ice on the roads.'

hurt in pain and not able to move

Tom and Anastasia sit in the back of the van. Anastasia is angry. 'Be careful,' says Tom quietly. 'These people are **dangerous**.'

Suddenly, the van **skids** on the ice and snow.

It goes off the road and hits a tree with a **crash**!

After a minute, Rita opens the back doors. 'Max?' she shouts.
'I – I can't get out!' Max shouts.

'Get out!' Rita tells Tom and Anastasia.

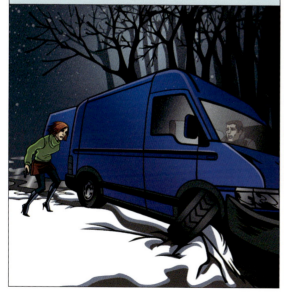

Tom gets out of the van and helps Anastasia. 'Are you OK?' Tom asks. 'Oh, sure!' Anastasia says.

dangerous that can kill you

skid to move without control when going over ice

crash a big noise when a car hits something and stops suddenly

READING CHECK

Correct the mistakes.

a Jodie-Anne and Anastasia come in a ~~small~~ *big* black car.

b The bodyguard shoots Joe in the arm.

c Max drives away slowly.

d Rita is worried about ice on the van.

e Anastasia feels happy.

f Tom and Anastasia are in the front of the van.

g The van hits a house.

h Rita can't get out of the van.

WORD WORK

1 **Find seven more words from Chapter 5 in the word square.**

S K I D M C T V N
B W P A G R E A T
S Y T N U A S Q S
H O S G Z N C K H
O G I E K H R E O
U H U R T R E N O
T C V O S P A L T
S M F U F Y M Z S
C R A S H T U Q O

2 Use the words from Activity 1 to complete the sentences.

a Some cars drive very fast in the winter and they . . . . . *skid* . . . . . on the ice.

b He can't talk quietly, he always . . . .

c 'Do you like that book?' 'Yes, it's . . . .'

d 'Call a doctor. Two people are . . . .'

e In the movie the man takes out a gun and he . . . . at the police.

f Some people open their mouths and . . . . when they are afraid.

g This is a . . . . place to walk across the road; cars drive past here very fast.

h When a car hits a tree you can hear a big . . . .

GUESS WHAT

What happens in the next chapter? Tick one box.

a Jodie-Anne gives three million dollars to the kidnappers.

c Anastasia runs away but the kidnappers shoot Tom.

b Jodie-Anne finds the blue van and she shoots Rita.

d Anastasia and Tom escape from the kidnappers. The police arrive.

CHAPTER 6

'Max!' Rita shouts. 'Are you OK?'

'I – I can't move,' he tells her.
'My legs! I can't move my legs.'

Suddenly, Tom **jumps** on Rita. He
knocks the gun from her hand.
'Run!' he shouts to Anastasia.

Tom runs after Anastasia.
'I'm behind you!' he shouts.

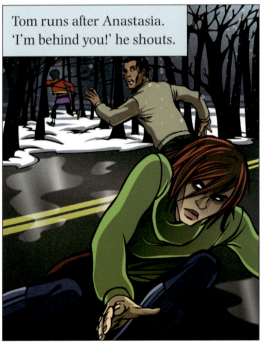

'Stop!' Rita shouts, and she
gets her gun.

jump to move suddenly from one
place to a different place

knock to hit strongly

Tom and Anastasia run through the trees. Rita has her gun again, and runs after them.

Then, Anastasia falls down in the snow. 'Ow!' she cries.

Tom helps Anastasia. Rita is getting **closer** and closer. 'Stop!' she shouts. 'Or I shoot!'

Rita shoots at them, but she doesn't hit Tom or Anastasia.

close near

'Down here!' Tom tells Anastasia. 'We can go across the **river** on the **bridge**.'

Tom and Anastasia run across the bridge, but Rita is close behind them.

Suddenly, Tom **slips** on the ice on the bridge.

Tom falls into the river and begins to **swim**. 'Go on!' he shouts to Anastasia.

river water that moves in a long line

bridge people can go across a river on this

slip to fall suddenly on ice

swim to go through the water moving your arms and legs

Rita stops on the bridge and gets ready to shoot Tom. Quickly, Anastasia gets some snow and makes a **snowball**.

She throws the snowball at Rita and . . .

. . . hits her on the head.
'Ow!' Rita shouts.

Rita falls into the river. 'Help!' she screams. 'Help me! I can't swim!'

Tom gets out of the water, and sees Rita in the river.
'Come on!' Anastasia shouts.
'But we can't leave her – she can't swim. We must help her,' Tom says.
'Are you kidding? She wants to kill us. Come on,' screams Anastasia.

snowball a ball that you make with snow and can throw at someone

'**Freeze!**' shouts a **police officer**.

Suddenly lots of police officers come running across the bridge.
They get Rita out of the river, and they **push** Tom to the **ground**.

'Wait!' says Anastasia. 'He's helping me – he's a good guy.'

'OK, OK, let's go to a warmer place,' says the police officer.
'You can tell us everything there.'

'Wait a minute. I don't understand. How ... Why are you here?'
Anastasia asks the police officer.

'You have a very good bodyguard. He's fast with his gun and with his cell phone. And when someone calls the police we move fast, too.'

freeze not to move

police officer a man or a woman that works for the police

push to move something quickly and strongly with your hands

ground we walk on this

The police take Tom, Anastasia and Rita back to their car.

'You sure can throw well, Anastasia!' Tom says. Anastasia laughs. 'I play **baseball** with the boys at my school,' she says. 'I'm the **pitcher**.' Tom laughs, too. 'You're great!' he says.

Back at home, Tom looks at his comic strip.
'How do the friends escape? Easy! Now I know!' thinks Tom.
'Sometimes real life can give you great ideas for a comic strip,' he laughs.

baseball a game that lots of people play in America; one person throws a ball and another person hits it with a bat

pitcher the person in a baseball team that throws the ball

READING CHECK

Match the two parts of these sentences.

a	Max can't . . .	**1**	run across the bridge.
b	Rita . . .	**2**	fall in the river.
c	Anastasia . . .	**3**	move his legs.
d	Tom and Rita . . .	**4**	runs after Tom and Anastasia.
e	Rita can't . . .	**5**	throw well.
f	Tom wants to . . .	**6**	finish his comic strip.
g	The police . . .	**7**	swim.
h	Anastasia can . . .	**8**	falls in the snow.
i	Now Tom can . . .	**9**	help Rita.

WORD WORK

1 Find words from Chapter 6 in the snow.

a j<u>ump</u>

b p _ _ _

c g _ _ _ _ _

d s _ _ _ _ _ _

e s _ _ _

f f _ _ _ _ _

g c _ _ _ _

h k _ _ _ _

2 Use the words from Activity 1 to complete the sentences.

a

Help!

Quickly! . . . . to the . . . . !

b

Please don't throw that . . . . ! You're standing very . . . .

c

Quick run! It's the police. . . . . !

. . . . !

d

Be careful! Don't . . . . my arm!

e

I can't open the door.

You must . . . . it.

f

Be careful. Don't . . . . There's a lot of ice.

PROJECT A   *Map Reading*

1 **The girl at the gas station gives Tom some directions to Hillside school in Bridgewater. Read the directions and follow the map. Which number is Hillside school?**

Go out of the gas station, turn left, and go straight on. When you come to the intersection, turn left. Go past the train station on the right, and go over the first crossroads into Bridgewater. Go past the video store on the left and the bookstore on the right. At the next crossroads turn right. Go down the hill past the hotel. Take the second road on the left. Go over the bridge and turn right. Hillside School is on your left.

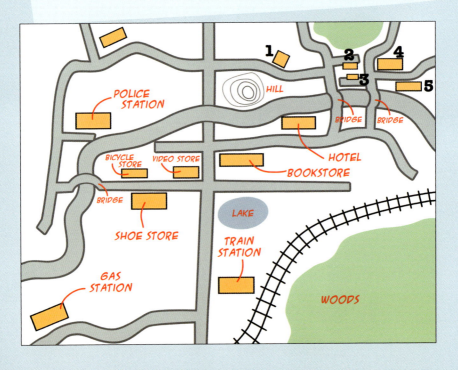

2 Look at the map again. Here are the directions from the train station to the police station in Bridgewater. Complete the directions with the words in the box.

crossroads   first   left   intersection

over   past   right   straight on

Go out of the train station, turn **(a)**........... and go **(b)**........... into Bridgewater. At the first **(c)**........... turn left. Go **(d)**........... the shoe store on the left and the bicycle store on the right. Then go **(e)**........... the bridge. When you come to the **(f)**........... turn right. Then take the **(g)**........... road on the right. You can see the police station on your **(h)**........... .

3 Draw a map and write down the directions from your home to your school, or another place near you. Use the phrases in Activities 1 and 2 to help you.

PROJECT B   *Writing a Comic Script*

1 Look at the comic strip in Activity 3. What chapter of *Kidnap!* is this from?

2 What does Tom say in the comic strip? Arrange his words.

a   is   coffee   terrible!   This

     no   in   There's   it!   sugar

....

b   sorry!   very   I'm

....

c   sit   I   here   Can   ?

....

d   sugar   Is   any   there   ?

....

e   coffee   white   I   please   have   Hi!   a   Can   ?

....

f   Here   are.   you   Thanks.

....

3 Write Tom's words in the correct pictures to complete the comic strip.

4 Here's a scene from *Kidnap!* that isn't in the book. Complete the words and pictures in the comic strip.

5 Choose another scene from *Kidnap!* that isn't in the book. Make it into a comic strip. Write the words and draw the pictures.

GRAMMAR CHECK

Information questions and question words

We use question words in information questions.

How do the two friends escape?

Where can I get a cup of coffee?

Why are you driving slowly?

We answer these questions by giving some information.

They run away through the trees.

In the coffee shop in the bookstore.

Because there is a lot of snow on the road.

1 **Write questions for the answers. Use a question word and the correct form of the verb.**

a (the story / take place)

   When does the story take place?

   In winter.

b (Tom / live) ....

   In America.

c (Tom / go out) ....

   Because he needs an idea for his comic strip.

d (Tom / go) ....

   To the bookstore in Harper.

e (Tom / go to Harper) ....

   By car.

f (Tom / find in the bookstore) ....

   Some paper.

g (he / draw) ....

   A woman with red hair.

h (the woman / stand in street) ....

   Because there's something wrong with her car.

i (they / see on the paper) ....

   They can see a map.

GRAMMAR CHECK

Modal auxiliary verbs: can, can't, and must

We use *can* + infinitive without *to* to talk about things that we are able to do or that are possible.

Can I help you? You can use my cell phone.

We use *can't* + infinitive without *to* to talk about things that we are not able to do or that are not possible.

There are no street names. We can't find the school.

We use *must* + infinitive without *to* to talk about things that we have to do or that are an obligation.

There's ice on the road. You must drive carefully.

2 **Choose the correct word to complete the sentences about Chapter 2.**

a This is important. We **can/must** phone the police.

b **Can/Must** I see the map? Maybe I **can/ must** find the school.

c When Tom and Rita get to the school they **can/can't** ask the teachers.

d Jodie-Ann Ryan **can't/must** go to the holiday concert at her old school.

e Anastasia **can/must** go to the school concert with her mother. She **can/can't** stay at home.

f They **can/can't** take Rita's car because there's something wrong with it.

g Tom and Rita **can/must** go quickly. There's only one hour before the kidnap.

h Famous people **can/can't** have a bodyguard.

i Tom is an artist so he **can/can't** draw well.

j Tom needs an idea because he **can/can't** finish his comic strip.

GRAMMAR

GRAMMAR CHECK

Imperatives

We use the infinitive without *to* for affirmative imperatives. We use imperatives to give instructions or orders.

Drive carefully on the ice.　　　　　*Wait* near the school.

Negative imperatives start with do not or don't + infinitive without *to*.

Don't ask questions.　　　　　*Don't be* late.

3 **Complete the sentences with the imperative form of the verbs in the box.**

drive	hurry	look	not lose	move
stop	take	think	wait	not worry

a Hurry.! There isn't much time.

b .... of all the money. .... about a thing.

c .... down the road for five kilometres. Then

.... at the place on the right.

d .... in the parking place and .... quickly

when you see the long, black car.

e .... my map – .... it!

f .... at this magazine. Do you know this woman?

4 **What does Rita tell Max? Complete her directions.**

be	call	drive	not drive	get
look	not lose	not shoot	use	wait

Here's the map. a) Look. at it carefully and

b) .... it. c) .... down

road 57 and d) .... near the school.

e) .... me when you get there. There's ice on

the road so f) .... fast. When the black car

arrives g) .... the girl out of the car.

h) .... your gun but i) .... And

j) .... careful. The bodyguard has a gun, too!

GRAMMAR CHECK

Present Continuous: affirmative and negative

We use the Present Continuous to talk about things that are happening now.

We make the Present Continuous affirmative with the verb **be** + the **–ing** form of the verb.

Tom's running to the car.   *Max and Joe are waiting near the school.*

We put **n't** (**not**) with the verb **be** to make the Present Continuous negative.

Rita isn't calling the police.   *They aren't driving fast.*

We make the **–ing** form of the verb by adding **–ing** to the infinitive without *to*. When verbs end in –e, we lose the e and add **–ing**.

smile – smiling   *drive – driving*

When short verbs end in consonant + vowel + consonant, we double the final consonant and add **–ing**.

run – running   *kid – kidding*

5 **Complete the sentences with the Present Continuous form of the verb in brackets. Then order the sentences to re-tell Chapter 4.**

a ☐ 'They want to kidnap Jodie-Ann Ryan's daughter – I .... (not kid)!' says Tom.

b ☐ 'Who is Rita calling?' asks Tom. 'Oh, no! She .... (phone) the kidnappers.'

c ☐ 'Tom's running (run) to the car. It must be important,' thinks Rita.

d ☐ Rita gets in the car with a gun. She .... (smile) but it isn't a nice smile.

e ☐ Tom's phone .... (not work), so Rita goes to the shop to call.

f ☐ 'The police .... (not come),' says Rita. 'My friends .... (wait) for us.'

g ☐ 'We must call the police. The kidnappers .... (wait) at Hillside School in Bridgewater,' says Tom.

h ☐ Tom .... (wait) in the car. He finds Rita's cell phone.

GRAMMAR CHECK

Present Simple: third person –s

We add –s to the infinitive without *to* to make the third person (*he/she/it*) form of the Present Simple.

Tom stops behind a blue van.   *A big black car comes down the road.*

When verbs end in –o, –ch, –ss, or –sh, we add –es to make the third person form.

finish – Tom finishes the picture of the woman.

When verbs end in consonant + –y, we change the y to i and add –es.

cry – cries

Some verbs are irregular.

say – says

We can use the Present Simple tense to re-tell a story.

6 Write the correct Present Simple form of the verbs in the brackets.

a 'Give me the girl!' 'Give me the girl!' Max shouts. (Max / shout)

b 'No, please don't take her.' .... (Jodie-Ann / scream)

c 'Get into the van.' .... (Rita / tell / Anastasia)

d 'Be careful, Joe!' .... (Max / shout)

e 'My leg!' .... (Joe / scream)

f 'Drive!' .... (Rita / tell / Max)

g 'Be careful. They're dangerous.' .... (Tom / say)

h 'Get out!' .... (Rita / tell / Tom and Anastasia)

i 'Are you OK?' .... (Tom / ask)

j 'Oh, sure!' .... (Anastasia / say)

GRAMMAR

GRAMMAR CHECK

Prepositions and prepositional verbs

Prepositions of movement tell us how something moves.

across   into   off

on   out of   through

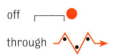

Some verbs can take a preposition. You can understand many verbs with prepositions from the meaning of the separate words.

look at   *run* after   *fall* down   *take* back   *go* out of   *get* in   *get* up

Some verbs + prepositions have a special meaning.

come on (= hurry)   *go* on (= don't stop)   *look* for (= try to find)

7 **Complete the sentences about Chapter 6 with the prepositions in the box. Use some prepositions more than once.**

across	after	back	down	for
into	on	~~out of~~	through	to	up

a Tom jumps on Rita and he knocks the gun <u>out of</u> her hand.

b Rita gets .... quickly and finds her gun.

c Tom and Anastasia run .... the trees. Rita runs .... them.

d Anastasia falls .... in the snow and Tom helps her to get

....

e Tom and Anastasia run .... the bridge. Tom slips .... the ice and he falls .... the river.

f Anastasia throws a snowball at Rita and hits her .... the head. Rita falls .... the river, too.

g Tom gets .... the river and looks .... Rita. She can't swim.

h Suddenly lots of police officers arrive. They are looking .... Anastasia. The police take Rita, Tom, and Anastasia back to their car.

i When Tom gets .... home he has lots of ideas for his comic strip.

GRAMMAR CHECK

Negative statements

We make the negative by adding **not** after the auxiliary verb **do/does** in the Present Simple.

Tom **doesn't** *(does not) work in an office.*

We add **not** after the verbs *be* or *can*.

Rita **isn't** *(is not) an artist.*

Tom **can't** *(cannot) finish his comic strip at first.*

We usually use the contracted form **–n't**.

8 Write the negative form of the verbs in *italics*.

a Anastasia *wants* to go to the holiday concert with her mother.

   Anastasia doesn't want to go to the holiday concert with her mother.

b Tom *knows* how to finish his comic strip.

   ....

c Max and Joe are leaving the bookstore. They *are drinking* coffee.

   ....

d Tom *gives* the paper back to the man.

   ....

e The woman's car *is* working.

   ....

f Joe *has* his map. He's happy about the plan.

   ....

g Hillside School *is* far from the shop.

   ....

h Rita goes into the shop. She *calls* the police.

   ....

i The bodyguard *can* stop the van.

   ....

j Max *can get* out of the van.

   ....

DOMINOES THE STRUCTURED APPROACH TO READING IN ENGLISH

Dominoes is an enjoyable series of illustrated classic and modern stories in four carefully graded language stages – from Starter to Three – which take learners from beginner to intermediate level.

Each *Domino* reader includes:
- **a good story** to read and enjoy
- **integrated activities** to develop reading skills and increase active vocabulary
- **personalized projects** to make the language and story themes more meaningful
- **seven pages of grammar activities** for consolidation.

Each *Domino* pack contains a reader, plus a MultiROM with:
- **a complete audio recording of the story**, fully dramatized to bring it to life
- **interactive activities** to offer further practice in reading and language skills and to consolidate learning.

If you liked this Starter Level *Domino*, why not read these?

The Big Story
John Escott

'Bring me something new and exciting. Bring me a BIG story!' says Rosie's editor at The Record newspaper.

And, when she leaves the office, Rosie does find a story. A story that is bigger than she expects. A story that takes her across Europe, into a dangerous world of art and art thieves.

Book ISBN: 978 0 19 424710 8
MultiROM Pack ISBN: 978 0 19 424674 3

Journey to the Centre of the Earth
Jules Verne

In Hamburg, Germany, Professor Otto Lidenbrock comes home with an old Icelandic book. In it there is a message about a journey to the centre of the Earth. This is the beginning of one of Jules Verne's most exciting stories.

'Is this message true? We must go to Iceland and see!' says Lidenbrock excitedly. But his nephew, Axel, wants to stay at home.

Can Lidenbrock and Axel – and their Icelandic guide, Hans – find the centre of the Earth? And can they all get back alive after their many underground adventures?

Book ISBN: 978 0 19 424718 4
MultiROM Pack ISBN: 978 0 19 424682 8

You can find details and a full list of books in the *Dominoes* catalogue and Oxford English Language Teaching Catalogue, and on the website: www.oup.com/elt

Teachers: see www.oup.com/elt for a full range of online support, or consult your local office.

	CEF	Cambridge Exams	IELTS	TOEFL iBT	TOEIC
Starter	A1	YLE Movers	–	–	–
Level 1	A1–A2	YLE Flyers/KET	3.0	–	–
Level 2	A2–B1	KET-PET	3.0-4.0	–	–
Level 3	B1	PET	4.0	57-86	550